THE TRAGEDY OF
LITTLE BIGHORN

THE TRAGEDY OF
LITTLE BIGHORN
WARREN J. HALLIBURTON

Franklin Watts
New York / London / Toronto / Sydney
A First Book / 1989

Photographs courtesy of:
Custer Battlefield Historical & Museum Association: pp.
8, 58 (top and middle), 59; The Granger Collection: pp.
13, 14 (bottom left), 17, 20, 27, 32, 38, 39, 46, 47, 50, 53, 58
(bottom); Smithsonian Office of Anthropology, Bureau
of American Ethnology: p. 14 (top left); Museum of the
American Indian: p. 14 (top right); Library of Congress:
cover, pp. 14 (bottom right), 41; South Dakota State Historical Society: pp. 33, 37.

Library of Congress Cataloging in Publication Data

Halliburton, Warren J.
The tragedy of Little Bighorn/Warren J. Halliburton.
p.   cm. — (A First book)
Bibliography: p.
Includes index.
Summary: Describes the impact of the westward migration of the
white settlers on the Indians of the Great Plains which culminated
in the massacre of Custer and his men in the battle at Little Big
Horn in 1876.
ISBN 0-531-10685-3
1. Little Big Horn, Battle of the, 1876 — Juvenile literature.
2. Custer, George Armstrong, 1839-1876 — Juvenile literature.
3. Indians of North America — Juvenile literature.   [1. Little Big
Horn, Battle of the, 1876.   2. Custer, George Armstrong. 1839-1876.
3. Indians of North America.]   I. Title.   II. Series.
E83.876.H28   1989
973.8'2 — dc19   88-30340   CIP   AC

CONTENTS

Introduction
9

Chapter One
Disturbances on the Great Plains
11

Chapter Two
Plans for a Bold Winter Campaign
16

Chapter Three
Hail the Conquering Hero
22

Chapter Four
Violations of Trust
30

Chapter Five
Toward Little Bighorn
35

Chapter Six
Custer's Last Stand
43

Epilogue
55

For Further Reading
62

Index
63

THE TRAGEDY OF
LITTLE BIGHORN

INTRODUCTION

Dead men do tell tales. Mostly little secrets, these tales lie hidden, sometimes for years, even generations. Then an opportunity for fresh investigation arises, and new clues are found. Pieced together, they explain what happened.

The tragedy of Little Bighorn is such a tale. For over a hundred years, the real story of one of the most startling defeats in the military history of the United States lay buried. Marble headstones on the Great Plains of Montana pay silent tribute to the more than two hundred cavalrymen killed in battle on that memorable day, June 25, 1876. Why they fought, and were destined to die, is recorded history. But, much like the prairie on which the battle took place, the details remained covered in mystery.

Eyewitness accounts of the battle were suspected by historians to be Indian legend, and held doubtful. There was little other evidence to document the fight—that is, until recently when, in August 1983, a prairie fire scorched much of the land reserved as Custer Battlefield National Monument.

With most of the monument's 760 acres of buffalo grass now burned away, the National Park Service seized the opportunity to begin a study of the naked landscape, to excavate the articles of war used over one hundred years ago. By recording their locations, and interpreting their meaning, Park Service archeologists hoped to reconstruct the battle. Today, through their efforts, we have a more detailed accounting of Custer's Last Stand, one replacing legend and theory with the facts of research and investigation. As more evidence of the battle is unearthed, new information can be anticipated about this tragic event in American history.

1

DISTURBANCES ON THE GREAT PLAINS

The Great Plains was western land. Its mighty spread reached from Texas in the south to Canada in the north, and from the lower Missouri and Mississippi rivers in the east to the Rocky Mountains in the west. This land was also the home of 225,000 Indians, mostly Sioux. For generations they shared the Great Plains with Cheyenne, Arapahoes, Kiowas, and other tribes.

The first whites to venture into the area came in the sixteenth century as explorers. Others followed in the seventeenth century; they were mostly fur trappers and missionaries. The Indians welcomed them, and by the eighteenth century were sharing the land with these pioneers. Being few in number, the newcomers were no threat to the Indians. These whites and red men lived together in peace.

The United States government had acknowledged the Indians' property rights by treaty, believing the Plains was largely wasteland, and not likely to attract a large number of white settlers. It was simply too barren to farm and develop into communities.

The government figured wrong. A series of discoveries that evoked dreams of quick riches changed all that. Beginning with the Gold Rush of 1849, immigrants swept out of the east. They traveled west in caravans of covered wagons, and trespassed over Indian land. And they hunted, some more for reckless sport than for food. Slaughtering some fifteen million buffalo, these adventurers killed off most of the Indians' main source of food and clothing.

Treaties were all but forgotten to accommodate the increasing number of whites coming into the area. Treaty violations led to violent encounters between the Indians and the whites.

In 1862, work began on a transcontinental railroad that would cross the Great Plains and bring in even more settlers. If the red man had ever doubted the deceit of the white man, the evidence could no longer be denied. The invaders had to be stopped.

*Passengers and train
crew shooting buffalo
on the Plains*

Sitting Bull of the Hunkpapa Sioux, Chief Joseph of the Nez Percé, Gall of the Hunkpapa Sioux, Geronimo of the Chiricahua Apache

[14]

The names of those Indians who led in the defense of their land are legendary: Sitting Bull, Crazy Horse, Chief Joseph, Cochise, Gall, and Geronimo. On the Oregon and Santa Fe trails, at Sand Creek, and along the South Platte River, they struck settlements in countless raids.

It was this show of Indian resistance and determination that led the federal government in 1868 to draw up yet another treaty, at Fort Laramie. The Dakota nation of Indians was granted all land now known as South Dakota as a Sioux reservation "forever." It included their most sacred hunting grounds, the Black Hills, and certain adjoining territory.

Those Indians willing to give up the fight accepted the conditions of reservation living. They became known as "friendlies," and lived under the supervision of government agencies.

Other Indians were not as easily satisfied. They refused what they saw as the white man's welfare, and chose to live their own way of life. Moving freely about the land outside the reservation, and feared by the white settlers, they became known as "hostiles."

2

PLANS FOR A
BOLD WINTER CAMPAIGN

At the time of the Treaty of Fort Laramie, General of the Army in the West was William T. Sherman. His assignment was to carry out the government's decision to protect the crews of workers completing the railroad. It was a mission he viewed as a military campaign. When this first transcontinental line was completed in 1869, Sherman joined in its official opening-day ceremonies.

He regarded the completion of the railroad as a victory over the "inferior" Indian, a mere animal, like the buffalo, standing in the way of a superior civilization. With plans underway to build branch lines that would cross more Indian land, Sherman knew that the military would continue to be needed to protect white migration west.

The uprisings continued, driving the general to warn the hostile Indians, "If you continue to fight,

*A tinted photograph of the ceremony that marked
the completion of the transcontinental railway
at Promontory Point, Utah, on May 10, 1869*

[17]

you will all be killed . . . live like white men, and we will help you all you want."

The Indians felt that the way of the whites was impossible, as well as undesirable, for their people. Chief Red Cloud of the Oglala Sioux answered, "We are on the mountains looking down on the soldiers and the forts. When we see the soldiers moving away, the forts abandoned, then I will come down and talk."

Promoted to General of the Army, Sherman was replaced in his western command by Gen. Philip H. Sheridan. He was of the same mind as his commanding officer. Sheridan had denounced the Indian as "a lazy, idle vagabond." The sooner these tribes were under the control of the military, he felt, the better.

In the Northern Plains, hundreds of young Cheyenne, Arapahoes, and Sioux were striking at settlements, stagecoach stations, and wagon trains. In the south, a series of attacks by hostiles on settlers along the Arkansas River brought matters to a head. Giving chase to a band of young braves, Sheridan and his calvarymen failed to overtake them. In his frustration, Sheridan thought of an unusual plan: Why not strike the hostiles when they would least expect it—in winter. The army would "prosecute the war with vindictive earnestness against all hostile Indians, till they are obliterated or beg for mercy."

The idea won General Sherman's support. He figured that a major attack on the hostiles was a way to clear the way west.

The prospect of waging a military campaign in a region of such brutal winters was unheard of. Even Sheridan's Indian scouts and guides expressed doubts, insisting that the soldiers would surely perish in the cold blizzards of the Kansas plains.

Both Sheridan and Sherman agreed that such a campaign would require bold leadership. Only such a person could turn the risks of winter weather into an opportunity for victory. By attacking the Indians in their villages, army troops would hit them at their source of supplies, without which they could not long survive. The Indians would be forced onto the reservations the government had provided for them.

General Sheridan knew the person best suited to carry out such a daring mission. The officer was now a lieutenant colonel who had served under him during the Civil War, as well as in the West. His success in battle had made him a hero well

remembered by Sheridan, along with the rest of the nation.

His name was George Armstrong Custer, an officer the army had court-martialed several months earlier for deserting his post, excessive cruelty to his men, and illegally ordering deserters shot. Custer's defense was to justify his conduct, not to deny the charges. His sentence was a one-year suspension from the army without pay.

Custer was still under suspension when he was sent for by Sheridan. The general came straight to the point. After explaining his plan and strategy, he asked Custer what he thought. Custer's reply was brief: "How soon do I start?"

George Armstrong Custer,
about 1875

3

HAIL THE CONQUERING HERO

While training his men for the winter campaign, Custer was ordered to establish a supply base farther south in the heart of Indian territory. He was then to wait until the winter weather took its toll. Once the Indians' ponies were weakened from the cold and hunger, Custer was to strike.

The regiment departed from Fort Hays on November 12, 1868. It included twelve hundred troops, four scouts, four hundred wagons, and a military band. Six days later the regiment reached its destination, and staked out Camp Supply. Then, Custer left with eleven companies of 800 cavalrymen to seek and destroy enemy Indians.

They were one full day on the Plains when Custer instructed one of his officers to take three troopers and two Indian guides to scout ahead for

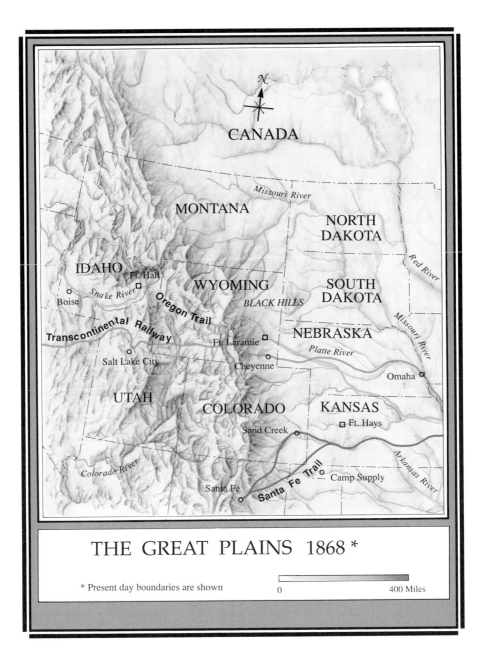

THE GREAT PLAINS 1868 *

* Present day boundaries are shown

0   400 Miles

enemy tracks. The officer was then to report by messenger any news of discovery.

The scouting party left at dawn. A foot of snow had fallen overnight, making travel slow but trailing easy. By midmorning a courier was already reporting back to Custer. They had found a trail. No more than twenty-four hours old, it was made by perhaps 150 Indians. Traveling south, they were probably headed for a village along the Washita River.

Custer instructed the messenger to rejoin his party and follow the trail until evening, then wait. He would join them and, using the darkness of night for cover, track down the Indians.

The mission proceeded according to plan. By sunset, the regiment had joined the scouting party and settled in a small, hidden ravine. Custer was prepared to attack. But his scouts discouraged the idea. They thought it best to wait until morning. The colonel dismissed their fears as nothing more than Indian ignorance and superstition.

Putting his plan into operation, Custer ordered the scouts to explore ahead. He kept his main body of troops a full quarter-mile behind. The precaution was to keep the noise of the horses on the crusted snow out of enemy range. The soldiers were also ordered to light no matches nor create any unnecessary disturbance.

By ten that evening, the scouts came upon the still-burning embers of a campfire, suggesting the presence of a village nearby. Once informed, Custer continued the advance, but with greater caution. Peering into the darkness of trees ahead, the troops watched and listened. Someone reported a herd, but was unable to determine whether it was horses or buffalo. A dog barked in the distance, and a bell tinkled. Not until they heard the cry of a baby were they certain they had come upon the village.

It was now past midnight, the men too weary to fight. Custer ordered the regiment divided into four units, each positioned on a different side of the village. The attack would begin at dawn.

The delay proved harder for Custer to bear than the bitter, cold night. The complaint of the Indian scouts was in not knowing the numbers of enemy braves lying in wait. They could not appreciate this white man's way of waging a battle with so little information. But the scouts worried alone and apart from the troops, cavalrymen who looked forward to the attack as an opportunity to make their mark with an impressive victory.

At dawn Custer ordered his cavalry to mount. They would lead the attack. But he worried that the enemy would hear their approach. Suddenly a rifle fired from the village. They had been discovered! Custer ordered the band to play "Garryowen," a popular song of rousing spirit.

It signaled the beginning battle. The cheers of cavalrymen echoed as a bugle sounded the charge. Guns cracking, the horsemen drove their mounts headlong into the village. Trampling tepees as they struck, the soldiers destroyed with blind rage. Men, women, and children scrambled for their lives. Some, escaping the slaughter, headed for the creek bank. A few jumped half-naked into the icy water of the Washita River. Others took cover behind stumps of trees and in sinkholes to avoid the rampaging soldiers.

By ten o'clock that morning, the raid was over and an uneasy peace enforced. Custer ordered a field hospital set up among the tepees. Riding in to check on the casualties, he counted one dead, one badly wounded officer, a third with minor injuries, and eleven wounded enlisted men.

Then he went to review the troops. They were now loosely assembled in a makeshift line just outside the village. As he approached, Custer noticed

*Custer leads the surprise attack on
the Cheyenne village on the Washita River.*

the number of Indians who had collected in the area, and his blood ran cold. Already outnumbered and low on ammunition, his men were in no condition to resume fighting. More critical was the fact they were being cut off from the ammunition wagon left behind.

For all his doubts and fears, Custer could still wonder where so many Indians had come from, and so quickly. Could it be the ignorant scouts were right, that in attacking the village, he had acted with more daring than wisdom?

Slowly, so as not to draw any notice, the commander turned his mount and stole back to the village. Once inside the clearing, he learned the awful truth. The village they were in was one of many in the area. Inhabited by Kiowas, Arapahoes, Comanche, and Apache, they were the homes of all the hostile Indians on the Plains. It was from these villages the Indians were arriving and gathering alongside the troops!

Custer was realizing the gravity of the situation when he was interruped by the ammunition wagon lunging into the village clearing. Its driver had managed to sneak past the Indians.

Momentarily relieved, the commander could think more clearly. There was not a moment to lose. He instructed that the women prisoners be given mounts. They would be used as hostages against enemy attack. The rest of the village he ordered destroyed. Then, in a show of bravado, the colonel led his troops and captives away. It was a convincing performance that worked! Once past the silently watching Indians, Custer led the cavalrymen and captives along the creek and in the direction of the next village. The observing Indians got the message. They rushed off to defend their homes.

It had just turned dark when Custer signaled a halt. Then, ordering an about-face, he led the expedition back over the same course it had just traveled. Passing through the burned-out village, they continued on across the dark plain. Not until 2:00 A.M., now safely away from the battlefield, did Custer dare stop to rest.

On the fourth day of their trip back, the Seventh Cavalry marched into Camp Supply, the regiment band playing "Garryowen" once again.

4

VIOLATIONS OF TRUST

Custer's victory at Washita in 1868 was not all glory. There were those who questioned the wisdom of the attack. They claimed that the slaughter was a mistake, that Washita Indians were friends who had influenced other Indians in signing peace treaties. The U.S. Bureau of Indian Affairs agreed. Even the military admitted that Custer had committed a tactical error. They censured the colonel for underestimating the number of Washita Indians and overestimating their hostility.

But the reputation of the now famous Indian fighter was established. And in the years that followed, Custer enjoyed the privileged treatment of an American hero. His everyday life as a military officer was frequently interrupted by personal invitations to honor his accomplishments on the field of battle. And when called upon to lead routine patrols, he often turned them into daring adventures. Assigned to round up renegade Indians, he narrowly escaped from more than one ambush. These experiences were instructive. They convinced this veteran soldier that when disciplined cavalry hit and hit hard, disorganized Indians fled.

As spiritual leader of the Hunkpapa Sioux (one of the seven tribes of Teton Sioux), Sitting Bull symbolized Indian resistance. As early as 1863, he had visited his woodland cousins, the Santees, on the reservation. It was where the white soldiers had said they were to live, up the Missouri where the soil was barren, wild game scarce, and the water unfit to drink. Sitting Bull remembered the pitiful conditions that took the lives of half the Santees during their very first winter on the reservation. He realized that the whites were taking the good land for themselves, and forcing the Indians to live on the unfit land of the reservation. The chief vowed he would never submit to such a condition.

By the following summer, Sitting Bull was fighting alongside the tribes of other Teton Sioux. It was to defend the women and children from the soldiers' attack. Soon after, the white chiefs sent the Tetons a message inviting them to a council of peace. Some Tetons went and signed a treaty. But

Hunting buffalo on the Plains;
Right: Sioux Indians in their winter
quarters among the willows.

Sitting Bull refused. He made camp west of the Black Hills along streams that ran into the Yellowstone. It was where the Powder, Tongue, Rosebud, and Bighorn rivers flowed through country rich with wild game. Sitting Bull settled here to live in peace with his people. He ignored the invitations of the white chiefs to join them in a treaty of peace.

When, in the autumn of 1868, they ordered his people, the Hunkpapas, to begin life as farmers on a reservation, Sitting Bull continued to ignore the summons. Other Indian leaders joined the chief in his camp. They decided what they had to do. It was to raid wagon trains and attack cavalry troops.

Realizing the great influence Sitting Bull had among his people, government officials renewed their appeal. They were ready to hold a council of peace. Sitting Bull welcomed the news. He also wanted peace, but only if it meant no more loss of Indian land or imprisonment of his people on reservations. Meanwhile, he continued to live with his people on land of his own choosing as his ancestors had done before him.

By the spring of 1874, relations between whites and Indians had worsened. More "friendlies" were deserting the reservations. They were sick and tired of the mistreatment and the rotten beef the white agents forced them to eat. Many joined Sitting Bull in his camp.

They had to be provided for. Camp supplies soon ran short, forcing the summer hunt for food to begin earlier than usual. It was while hunting buffalo that Sitting Bull heard the terrible news. The treaty of 1868 had been violated. The soldier Custer had invaded the land of the Indians in the Black Hills.

5 TOWARD LITTLE BIGHORN

The army's expedition into the Black Hills was prompted by General Sheridan's frustration over repeated Indian attacks. A largely unexplored region, the Black Hills served as an ideal hideout for hostile Indians. What better location than this, Sheridan reasoned, to build a fort.

But the Sioux considered the Black Hills sacred. In all treaty negotiations, they insisted that its mountains remain untouched.

Because sending a U.S. military expedition into the territory was a violation of the Treaty of Fort Laramie, Sheridan needed an excuse, one he could justify. He claimed that the truce was already broken by the Indians' refusal to report to their reservations. This defiance of the white man's law, he declared, was also demonstrated in Indian attacks on overland travelers. They were all the justification he needed to send troops into the area.

When Custer learned that he had been selected to lead the expedition, he was elated. The appointment was an opportunity not only to gain a higher rank but to win added recognition.

In the summer of 1874, the Seventh Cavalry made its way into the Black Hills of Dakota Territory. Although Custer's mission was to select a site upon which to build a fort, the expedition ended on a note of far greater significance. Several of Custer's men discovered gold.

It did not take long for reports of this find to filter back east. Soon, miners were invading the Black Hills. The sacred land of the Indians, trespassed by the military, was now being violated by speculators.

Word of the outrage spread among the tribes like wildfire. Now fully disgusted with the government's disregard of the treaty, Sioux, Cheyenne, and other tribes saw no reason to stay on the reservation. Many traveled north to the more traditional hunting grounds in Montana and the Dakotas. Others joined Sitting Bull who threatened war.

We have been deceived by the white people. . . .
The Black Hills country was set aside for the
Indian by Government treaty. It was ours by

Custer's 1874 invasion of the Black Hills, part of the Great Sioux Reservation under the treaty of 1868. In this photograph Custer's wagon train can be seen making its way down Castle Creek valley.

solemn agreement, and we made the country our home. Our homes in the Black Hills were invaded when gold was discovered there. Now, the Indian must raise his arm to protect his women, his children, his home; and if the Government lets loose an army upon us to kill without mercy, we shall fight as brave men fight. We shall meet our enemies and honorably defeat them, or we shall all of us die in disgrace.

Sioux scalp shirt of hide decorated with eagle feathers, beads, and human hair

Sioux Indian bows and arrows

Agency representatives warned Sitting Bull to lead his people to the reservations. The great chief answered, "We want only to be left alone."

His wish was not to be. Attracted by the promise of gold and riches, more prospectors flocked into the territory. They dug up the land and brought herds of cattle to graze on the buffalo grasslands. The government, seeing no way to keep them out, offered to buy the Black Hills from the Indians. But the sacred land was not for sale.

The Sioux not only felt insulted, but cheated. They continued to desert the reservations. Some took out their anger in raids on settlements. The situation worsened. By the winter of 1875, government officials informed Sitting Bull and others living outside the reservations that "they must return . . . before January 31, 1876; and that if they neglect or refuse so to move, they will be reported to the War Dept. as hostile Indians, and that a military force will be sent to compell them to obey the order of the Indian Dept."

Six days later the government issued an order for action. All Sioux and Cheyenne found off reservations were to be refused shelter and supplies. Those on reservations were to be immediately disarmed.

Sitting Bull had had enough. The spiritual leader called for a council of war. Attending the meeting were Sioux, northern Cheyenne, as well as warriors from tribes of eastern Sioux—ten to twelve thousand Indians in all.

The rumor of war was challenged by Eastern newspapers. GIVE US PHIL SHERIDAN read the headlines. The government responded. The general was given command and ordered to put down the Indian uprising. He immediately telegraphed his department commanders, Brig. Gen. George Crook in Omaha and Brig. Gen. Alfred H. Terry in St. Paul. They were to prepare for a spring offensive against the hostile Indians. Terry was also to inform Lt. Col. George Armstrong Custer to report to him for duty in this operation.

Sheridan, Crook, Terry, and Custer

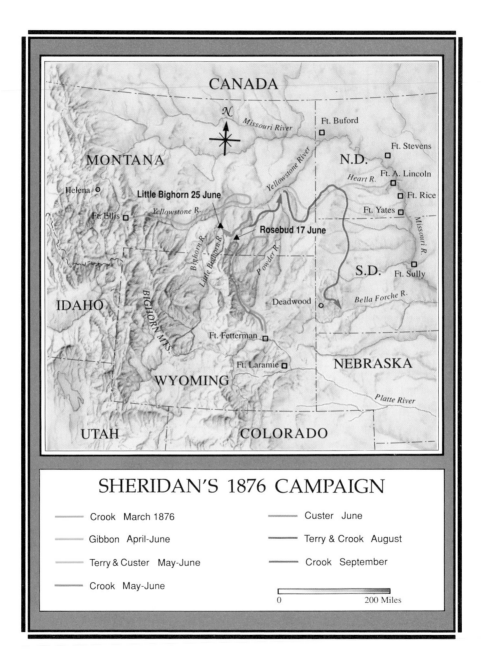

SHERIDAN'S 1876 CAMPAIGN

—— Crook   March 1876

—— Gibbon   April-June

—— Terry & Custer   May-June

—— Crook   May-June

—— Custer   June

—— Terry & Crook   August

—— Crook   September

0   200 Miles

6 CUSTER'S LAST STAND

On February 1, 1876, the government officially ordered U.S. troops to remove Indians from the western territory onto reservations. The machinery for tragedy was set in motion.

General Sheridan drew up a plan for a three-sided campaign. Col. John Gibbon, under Terry's command, was to march east from Fort Ellis, Montana. Terry himself was to head a second column, which included Custer, west from Fort Abraham Lincoln in North Dakota. And a third column, under the command of Crook, was to move north into Montana from Fort Fetterman in Wyoming. Converging from opposite directions, the troops would trap the Indians in the middle—or so it was planned.

The operation was no sooner underway when Terry was informed that Gibbon's scouts had sighted Indians gathering in the valley of the Tongue River. The general immediately assigned Maj. Marcus A. Reno six companies of the Seventh Cavalry to check out the report. It was confirmed.

On June 17, General Crook encountered Sioux resistance near Rosebud Creek in southern Montana. Facing defeat, he withdrew, returning with his men to Wyoming.

Neither Terry nor Gibbon was aware that the third column was out of action. With about 925 officers and men. Terry continued west up the Yellowstone River toward the Little Bighorn.

On June 21, Terry revealed his battle plan. Custer was to lead a regiment up the Rosebud, pick up the Indian trail, and "overhaul the Indians." He was also to meet up with Gibbon in five days. They were then to form a joint attack on June 26.

Custer was given command of twelve companies of the Seventh Cavalry and a detachment of Crow and Arikara scouts. He had refused a battalion of the Second Cavalry, along with a pair of rapid-fire Gatling guns. Having trained with many of the men, he believed them equal to any assignment, including the defeat of all the Indians of the Plains if it came to that. It was in this spirit that the colonel also ignored the warnings of his scouts that the Sioux and Cheyenne numbered many more than the eight hundred estimated by the Bureau of Indian Affairs.

Custer simply stressed the need for a surprise attack if they were to succeed. Otherwise the Indians would escape. For the next few days, the regiments proceeded with caution past the sites of three Indian villages, all recently deserted. On June 25, at 2:00 A.M., the soldiers made camp in a deep divide between Rosebud and Little Bighorn, and waited.

It was not quite daylight when Custer learned from scouts that they had discovered an Indian village less than fifteen miles away. When he demanded to know the number of Indians it contained, the scouts answered, "Enough Sioux to keep up fighting for two to three days." Custer greeted the news with a smile: "I guess we'll get through with them in one day."

As the regiment awaited orders, an officer learned that a pack mule had lost a box of hardtack (a type of biscuit made from flour and water). He sent a squad to hunt for it. But the hardtack had already been discovered by three Indians. The

Crazy Horse and Sitting Bull mounted before
their warriors at the Little Bighorn,
June 25, 1876. This pictograph was made by
Amos Bad Heart Bull, an Oglala Sioux.

A pictograph by Red Horse, a Sioux chief, of Custer's troops approaching the Indian village at Little Bighorn

[47]

troopers quickly drove them off, but when the incident was reported to Custer, he realized that the Indians now knew of their presence.

The advantage of a surprise attack suddenly gone, Custer made a fateful decision. He divided his forces into three battalions. Pointing to the southwest, he instructed Capt. Frederick W. Benteen to lead one battalion, consisting of about 125 men, in that direction, and, if the captain found the village, to "pitch in." Custer then ordered Major Reno to lead the second battalion of about 140 men down the south side of the divide. Custer would follow with his battalion of about 215 men on the north side. In this way, the Seventh Cavalry would advance toward Little Bighorn with all twelve companies. They would also have the Indians pinned down at Little Bighorn from three different directions.

As Custer advanced with his column, a scout reported that he had seen some forty Indians racing away on ponies. The village could not be far off, perhaps on the base of the Little Bighorn River which cut the plain ahead. Three miles later they came upon the Little Bighorn. There was still no village to be seen, only a small cloud of dust a mile downstream.

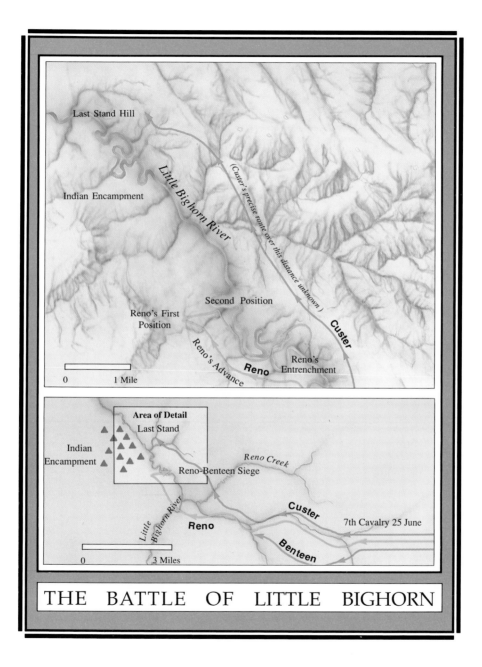

Last Stand Hill

Indian Encampment

Little Bighorn River

(Custer's precise route over this distance unknown)

Second Position

Reno's First
Position

Reno's Advance

Reno

Custer

Reno's
Entrenchment

0   1 Mile

Area of Detail
Last Stand

Indian
Encampment

Reno Creek

Reno-Benteen Siege

Little Bighorn River

Reno

Custer

Benteen

7th Cavalry 25 June

0   3 Miles

THE BATTLE OF LITTLE BIGHORN

Reno's column retreating

On Custer's orders, his adjutant, William W. Cooke, informed Reno that he was to lead the attack with the support of the entire outfit. He waited long enough to see Reno off, and then turned his mount to ride to where Custer waited with his company, about three-quarters of a mile up the divide. As he proceeded, Cooke heard a horse's hoofs pounding behind him. It was a scout bringing word from Reno that he had already met the Indians—lots of them!

No one knows whether Cooke relayed this information to Custer. History only records that Custer abruptly turned his troops from the divide and rode north. His plan, or so it seemed, was to attack the Indians as they fought Reno and his men.

Looking down on the mile-wide river bottom, his view hampered by trees, bluffs, and haze, Custer could barely make out Reno's line far to the left. But what he could plainly see beyond the trees was circle after circle of tepees—lodges of the northern Cheyenne, and of Oglala, Miniconjou, and Hunkpapa Sioux—probably the largest number of hostile Indians ever to gather on the Plains. Although Custer realized that the encampment was a large one, he didn't realize how large. Adding up to some two thousand, they outnumbered the troops twenty to one. Nor could any of the soldiers imagine that many of these Indians were armed with Winchester repeating carbines. Custer believed, with his men, only what he saw. A few ponies stood grazing as several squaws did their chores, moving quietly among the tents. The village seemed totally unprepared for attack. As Custer was heard to observe, "We've caught them napping."

He decided to attack before the Indians had a chance to escape. The master Indian fighter remembered that it was not the Indian's way to stand and fight, but to strike and escape. They would have to be taken by surprise. The strategy was one he had used in the past, and with repeated success.

Turning to his bugler, Custer said, "I want you to take a message to Captain Benteen. Ride fast as you can, and tell him to hurry. Tell him it's a big village, and I want him to be quick, and to bring the ammunition packs." Adjutant Cooke intercepted the bugler as he was leaving. He knew the young orderly was an Italian immigrant, and still learning English. Rather than risk confusion, Cooke wrote the following message:

Benteen: Come on. Big village. Be quick. Bring packs. W.W. Cooke, P.S. Bring packs.

Sioux warriors battling the Seventh Cavalry

Captain Benteen arrived with his forces some forty-five minutes later. They joined Reno and his men where they were, pinned on the hilltop. And for two days they fought off the Indians while wondering about Custer and what was keeping their commander from relieving them. Finally, troops under the command of generals Terry and Gibbon arrived, and quickly drove off the Indians now scattered in the hills.

A scout reported the news soon after. Colonel Custer and all his men lay dead on a ridge above the Little Bighorn.

They had no tales to tell. The only witnesses were the victors—the Indians.

EPILOGUE

The exact movements of Custer and his men during the battle of Little Bighorn remained obscure these many years. Stories—claimed to be eyewitness accounts—were reported soon after the event. They were related by Indians who had participated in the massacre. Many of them, weary of war, had settled for the peaceful existence of the reservation. Their statements, given to Indian agents about that fateful day, appeared in newspapers and journals. Many of these accounts were contradictory. Few were considered accurate. All were suspect, whether because of faulty translations, half truths, or correspondents' imaginations.

Recent studies of these reports, however, have revealed certain consistencies. Many of the claims have since been supported by archeological findings. In 1985, the National Park Service sent its own archeologists into the area to dig up the evidence. To date it includes about four thousand artifacts. Identification of where they were found, what they were, and how they were used became a full-fledged study. With the aid of metal detectors, sieves, and trowels, teams of examiners surveyed the old battleground. In this way some of the details of the battle were reconstructed, and new details of Custer's last hours introduced.

For example, spent rifle shells unearthed in the area confirm the fact that, in his final attack, Custer did move his men north along the high ground now known as Greasy Grass Ridge. Here he positioned a company of soldiers who were deployed into a broad arc formation facing south. Leaving a company between himself and them, Custer then took the three remaining companies along the land once known as Last Stand Hill.

It was here the soldiers were attacked from the south by Sioux, and from the north by more Sioux and Cheyenne. Standing their ground, the soldiers formed a broad V-shaped pattern, a typical battle formation. Angled north toward Last Stand Hill, the soldiers fought at long range. But, suffering heavy casualties, they soon found themselves surrounded and the enemy warriors closing in.

Evidence of this final battle was in the locations of cartridge cases fired. Unearthed from where they were embedded in the ground, these shells matched the cartridge cases issued to the soldiers of the Seventh Cavalry. They also revealed the soldiers' positions.

The most intense Indian fire was evidently from a distance of about 300 feet southeast of where the soldiers had assumed their arc formation. Bullets corresponding to the calibers of cartridge cases identified as Indian were found in army positions. They indicate the soldiers were probably overrun by Indians bearing heavy firearms.

Some of the weapons used by these Indians were later fired at Custer's cavalry line. They indicate that, as the Sioux and Cheyenne warriors moved upslope on Last Stand Hill, other Indians had joined forces at a knoll north and east of the hill. From this vantage point, they shot down into the knot of remaining cavalry. Emptying their firearms, the soldiers fought on. In the hand-to-hand combat that followed, those remaining were quickly overwhelmed. Using hatchets and clubs, the Indians completed the massacre.

When accounts of Little Bighorn were published in eastern newspapers, people were stunned. The

Cavalry boot uncovered at the archeological dig in 1985. The top had been cut off by a Sioux or Cheyenne Indian, as had virtually every boot found at the site. The Indians later used the tops to make satchels.

Right: A human finger bone with wedding ring in the exact position they were found by archeologists. Below: Human vertebra with metal arrowhead from the Little Bighorn battle site.

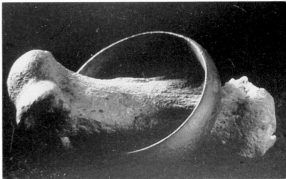

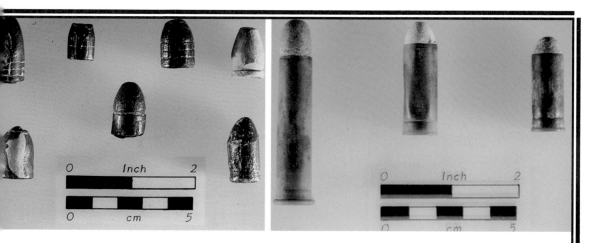

Left: Spent bullets from a variety of guns used by Sioux and Cheyenne warriors. Right: Cartridges from 45–caliber Springfield carbine and 45–caliber Colt revolver used by the Seventh Cavalry.

Using technology borrowed from forensic osteology, a skull fragment found on the battlefield was matched to a portrait of Miles O'Hara, a soldier known to have fought under Custer.

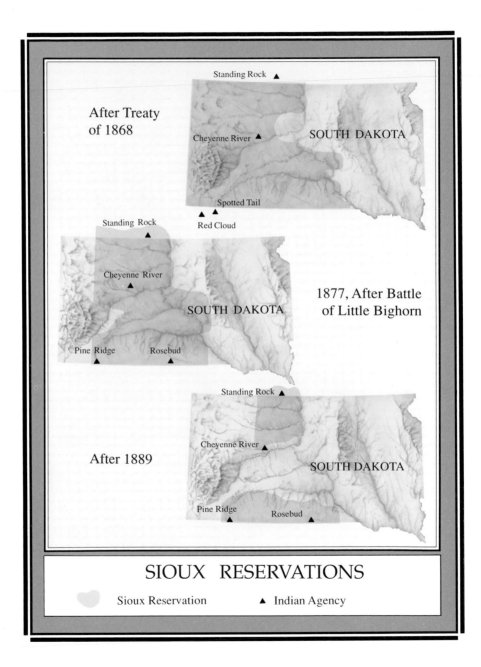

After Treaty
of 1868

Standing Rock ▲

Cheyenne River ▲

SOUTH DAKOTA

Spotted Tail
▲ ▲
Red Cloud

Standing Rock
▲

Cheyenne River
▲

SOUTH DAKOTA

1877, After Battle
of Little Bighorn

Pine Ridge   Rosebud
▲   ▲

Standing Rock ▲

Cheyenne River ▲

After 1889

SOUTH DAKOTA

Pine Ridge
▲   Rosebud
▲

SIOUX RESERVATIONS

Sioux Reservation   ▲ Indian Agency

story of the death of Custer and the decimation of the Seventh Cavalry provoked a public outcry. Sheridan immediately ordered more troops west to hunt down and kill the Sioux and their Cheyenne allies. Not only did Little Bighorn bring to a close the life of an American hero, but, in time, the end of a great culture as well, that of the Plains Indians.

FOR FURTHER READING

Bleeker, Sonia. *The Sioux Indians.* New York: William Morrow, 1962.

Flatley, Dennis R. *The Railroads: Opening the West.* New York: Franklin Watts, 1989.

Marrin, Albert. *War Clouds in the West: Indians & Cavalrymen. 1860–1890,* New York: Atheneum, 1984.

McGovern, Ann. *If You Lived with the Sioux Indians.* New York: Four Winds, 1974.

McGraw, Jessie Brewer. *Chief Red Horse Tells About Custer: The Battle of the Little Bighorn, an Eyewitness Account Told in Indian Sign Language.* New York: Dutton, 1981.

Utley, Robert M. *Custer Battlefield National Monument.* Historical Handbook Series No. 1. Washington, D.C.: National Park Service, 1969.

————. *Indian, Soldier, and Settler: Experiences in the Struggle for the American West.* The Gateway Series. St. Louis: Jefferson National Expansion Historical Association, 1979.

INDEX

Amos Bad Heart Bull, 46
Apache, 14, 28
Arapahoes, 11, 18, 28
Archeologists, 10, 55–56, 58
Arikara scouts, 44
Arkansas River, 18

Benteen, Frederick W., 48, 52, 54
Bighorn River, 33
Black Hills, 15, 33, 34, 35–37
   Gold, 36, 39
Buffalo, 12, 13, 32
Bureau of Indian Affairs, 45

Camp Supply, 22, 29
Castle Creek valley, 37

Cheyenne, 11, 27, 36, 45, 61
   Little Bighorn, 56–57, 58
   Raids, 18
Chief Joseph, 14, 15
Chief Red Cloud, 18
Chiricahua, 14
Cochise, 15
Comanche, 28
Cooke, William V., 51, 52
Council of peace, 34
Council of war, 40
Crazy Horse, 12, 15, 46
Crook, George, 40, 41, 43–44
Crow scouts, 44
Custer Battlefield National Monument, 10

Custer, George Armstrong, 20, 41
   Black Hills, 34, 36–37
   Hero, 10, 30–31
   Last stand, 44–55
   Little Bighorn, 48, 51–52, 54, 55–57, 61
   Uprising, 40
   Washita, 24–29, 30
   Winter campaign, 19, 21, 22, 24–29

Dakota nation, 15

Fort Abraham Lincoln, 43
Fort Ellis, 43
Fort Fetterman, 43

Fort Hays, 22
Fort Laramie, 15, 16, 35
Friendlies, 15
Fur trappers, 11

Gall, 14, 15
Geronimo, 14, 15
Gibbon, John, 43, 44, 54
Gold, 12, 36, 39
Greasy Grass Ridge, 56
Great Plains, 9
    Area included in, 11
    Gold Rush, 12
    Indians in, 11

Hostiles, 15, 18, 28, 35, 40, 51
Hunkpapa, 14, 31, 34, 51

Kiowas, 11, 28

Last Stand Hill, 56, 57
Little Bighorn, 9, 10, 45–48, 55–61

Miniconjou, 51
Missionaires, 11

National Park Service, 10, 56
Nez Percé, 14

Northern Cheyenne, 51

Oglala, 18, 46, 51
Oregon trail, 15
O'Hara, Miles, 59

Powder River, 33

Raids, 15, 18, 39
Railroad, 12, 16, 17
Red Horse, 47
Reno, Marcus A., 44, 48, 50, 51, 54
Reservations, 31, 36
    Friendlies, 15
    Mistreatment of Indians on, 34
Rosebud Creek, 44–45
Rosebud River, 33

Sand Creek, 15
Santa Fe trail, 15
Santees, 31
Scalp shirt, 38
Second Cavalry, 44
Seventh Cavalry, 44, 48, 53, 57, 61
    Gold discovered by, 36
Sheridan, Philip H., 18, 35, 40, 41, 43, 61
    Winter campaign, 18–19, 21, 22

Sherman, William T., 16, 18, 19
Sioux, 11, 33, 36, 40, 45, 51, 61
    At Battle of Little Bighorn, 53, 56–57, 58
    Black Hills, 35
    Raids, 18, 39
    Red Horse, 47
    Reservations, 39–40
    Scalp shirt, 38
    see also Hunkpapa
    see also Oglala
Sitting Bull, 12, 14, 31, 36, 38, 40, 46
    Reservation, 31, 33, 34, 39–40
South Platte River, 15

Terry, Alfred H., 40–41, 43–44, 54
Teton, 31
Tongue River, 33, 44
Treaties, 12, 15, 16, 35

U.S. Bureau of Indian Affairs, 30

Washita, 24–26, 28–29, 30

Yellowstone River, 44